THE LIBRARY OF
MEDIEVAL TIMES

Medieval Food and Customs

Stuart A. Kallen

ReferencePoint
Press®

San Diego, CA

About the Author

Stuart A. Kallen is the author of more than 250 nonfiction books for children and young adults. He has written on topics ranging from the theory of relativity to the art of animation. In addition, Kallen has written award-winning children's videos and television scripts. In his spare time, he is a singer, songwriter, and guitarist in San Diego.

© 2015 ReferencePoint Press, Inc.
Printed in the United States

For more information, contact:
ReferencePoint Press, Inc.
PO Box 27779
San Diego, CA 92198
www.ReferencePointPress.com

LIBRARY OF CONGRESS CATALOGING-IN-PUBLICATION DATA

Kallen, Stuart A., 1955–
  Medieval food and customs / by Stuart A. Kallen.
    pages cm. — (The library of medieval times)
  Audience: Grades 9 to 12.
  Includes bibliographical references and index.
  ISBN-13: 978-1-60152-718-9 (hardback)
  ISBN-10: 1-60152-718-7 (hardback)
  1. Food habits—Europe—History—To 1500—Juvenile literature. 2. Cooking, Medieval—
Juvenile literature. 3. Europe—Social life and customs—Juvenile literature. I. Title.
  GT2853.E8K35 2015
  394.1'2094—dc23
                                                                    2014012140

CONTENTS

IMPORTANT EVENTS OF MEDIEVAL TIMES

800
In Rome, Pope Leo III crowns Charlemagne emperor; his Carolingian dynasty rules western Europe until 987.

1000
A century of invention in farming begins; devices such as the heavy plow increase agricultural productivity and help double Europe's population.

632
The Prophet Muhammad dies as Islam begins to expand both east and west of the Arabian Peninsula.

ca. 950
Europe's first medical school opens in Salerno, Italy.

1099
The First Crusade ends Muslim rule in Jerusalem until 1187, when the Muslims under Saladin recapture Jerusalem from the crusaders.

400	600	800	1000	1200

476
Romulus Augustulus, the last Roman emperor in the West, is dethroned.

1066
William of Normandy defeats the last Anglo-Saxon king at the Battle of Hastings, establishing Norman rule in England.

1200
The rise of universities begins to promote a revival of learning throughout the West.

1130
Church authorities in France ban tournaments; the ban on these popular festivals, which provide knights with opportunities to gain prestige and financial reward, is later reversed.

1184
Church officials meeting in Verona, Italy, approve burning at the stake as a punishment for anyone found guilty of heresy.

1215
King John of England signs the Magna Carta, limiting the rights of the monarchy.

1346
Using the longbow, English archers overwhelm the French army at the Battle of Crécy during the Hundred Years' War.

1328
Charles IV dies, ending 341 years of successful rule by the Capetian kings who established modern France.

1316
The Italian physician Mondino De' Luzzi writes the first book of the medieval period devoted entirely to anatomy.

1378
The Great Schism, in which there are three claimants to the papacy, occurs.

1250	1300	1350	1400	1450

1347
The deadly bubonic plague strikes Europe and returns intermittently for the next 250 years.

1337
The Hundred Years' War begins between France and England.

1453
The Ottoman Turks conquer Constantinople following a seven-week bombardment with cannons.

1267
Henry III of England enacts the Assize of Bread and Ale, one of the first laws to regulate the production and sale of food; the law ties the price of bread to the price of wheat, thus preventing bakers from setting artificially high prices.

1231
Pope Gregory IX establishes the "Holy Inquisition," whose purpose is to search out heretics and force them to renounce their views.

A Melding of Food and Cultures

In 1390 the first English cookbook, the *Forme of Cury* (or the *Proper Method of Cookery*), contained a recipe for ravioli: "Take fine flour and sugar and make pasta dough; take good cheeses and butter and cream them together; then take parsley, sage, and shallots, and chop them finely, and put them in the filling. Put the boiled [raviolis] on a bed of grated cheese and cover them with more grated cheese, and then reheat them."[1]

The simple ravioli recipe demonstrates the way various foods, farming practices, and cultures mixed in the medieval era, or Middle Ages. This period lasted from the fall of the Roman Empire in the fifth century to the beginning of the Renaissance in the mid-fifteenth century.

Butter and cheese were staples of northern Germany and Scandinavia. The foods were brought to England by Roman soldiers near the beginning of the medieval era. Sugar was first brought to the British Isles from the Middle East around 1099 by Christian crusaders returning from Jerusalem, where they waged holy war against Muslims who controlled the city.

The herbal ingredients used in the ravioli recipe, parsley and sage, are of Italian origin. The herbs were brought to Britain by the Normans, who occupied Sicily from 1091 to 1194 and conquered England during the period. Before the Normans, Sicily had been ruled by Arabs for more than four hundred years. During that time Arab traders introduced Europeans to Asian shallots, rice, saffron, cinnamon, and black pepper. The wheat for the flour was likely grown using new methods of agriculture first brought to Spain by North African Berbers during a seventh-century invasion. These farming practices, which spread across Europe, included intensive irrigation, the use of animal droppings for fertilizer, and improved plows.

Kings and Commoners

The *Forme of Cury* was compiled for English king Richard II. The ravioli recipe was likely enjoyed only by nobility and clergy who could afford costly foods such as sugar. During the medieval era the nobility made up about 3 percent of the population, and the clergy made up about 7 percent. The other 90 percent of the population were called peasants, serfs, or commoners. Each of these terms indicated that the person was a poor farmer who subsisted by working the land.

Collectively the nobility, clergy, and peasants were known as the divinely ordained orders. In this class system, each order had its own role as predetermined by God: The nobility owned the land and oversaw defenses on tiny, independent estates known as fiefdoms; the church was in charge of spiritual matters; and the peasants produced food for all for little or no profit.

During the first half of the medieval era, little money circulated. Most commodities not produced on individual fiefdoms were obtained by barter in small market towns. Craft workers who specialized in making farm implements, dishes, clothing, and other items were usually paid for their efforts in grain, beer, meat, textiles, or the free use of a small piece of farmland.

One group of people did not fit into the divinely ordained orders: merchants. Around the tenth century, traveling merchants and traders rapidly expanded commerce by securing trade routes through Italy. These routes connected Europe to the Middle East and Africa through shipping fleets on the Mediterranean Sea. Trade routes were supply lines for spices, wine, food, furs, clothing, glass, jewels, musical instruments, and other luxuries. The merchants grew rich, as did the rulers who taxed all trade.

WORDS IN CONTEXT

Crusades: a series of religious wars between 1095 and 1285 organized by European popes to depose the Muslim rulers of Jerusalem.

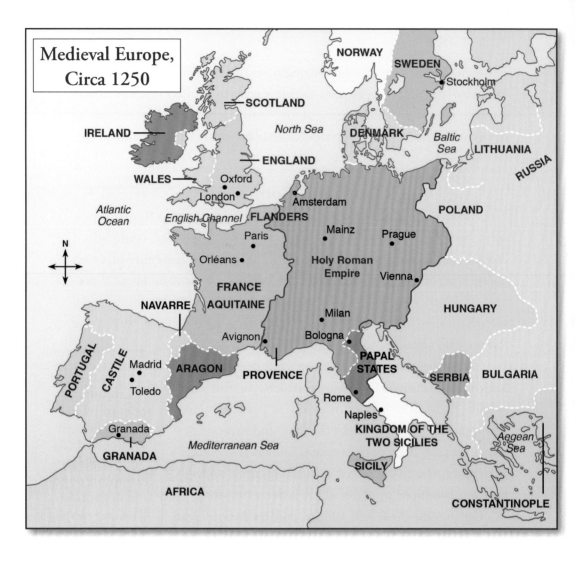

Medieval Europe, Circa 1250

NORWAY
SWEDEN
• Stockholm
SCOTLAND
North Sea
DENMARK
Baltic Sea
LITHUANIA
RUSSIA
IRELAND
ENGLAND
WALES
Oxford •
London •
Amsterdam
POLAND
Atlantic Ocean
English Channel
FLANDERS
Paris •
Mainz •
Prague •
Orléans •
Holy Roman Empire
Vienna •
FRANCE
NAVARRE
AQUITAINE
HUNGARY
Milan •
Avignon •
Bologna •
PAPAL STATES
PORTUGAL
CASTILE
Madrid •
ARAGON
PROVENCE
SERBIA
BULGARIA
Toledo •
Rome •
Granada •
Naples •
GRANADA
Mediterranean Sea
KINGDOM OF THE TWO SICILIES
Aegean Sea
SICILY
AFRICA
CONSTANTINOPLE
N

Spoiled Food, Plagues, and War

Although new foods and customs from foreign lands influenced European culture, they did not change the most basic aspects of life. Average Europeans during the medieval period rarely lived past the age of forty. About one-third of all children died before the age of five, and a significant number of women died during childbirth. Spoiled food, poor sanitation, disease, plagues, and warfare ensured life was brutal and short. In addition, widespread famines struck numerous times in every century throughout the Middle Ages.

Despite ongoing disasters, improved farming practices and nutrition kept the European population stable throughout most of the early medieval period. There was even a population boom between the eleventh and thirteenth centuries due to agriculture expanding into the wilderness and the introduction of the horse collar and horseshoe. In addition, the period between 950 and 1250 was known as the medieval warm period due to several centuries of unusually mild weather. The warm weather helped ease the burdens on those who depended on farming for their survival.

Darkness and Light

The medieval period was traditionally referred to as the Dark Ages since culture and economic well-being grew stagnant after the fall of the Roman Empire in the fifth century. However, historians now believe the term *Dark Ages* is inaccurate. Although existence during the medieval period was not comfortable by modern standards, life bore little resemblance to the harsh, crude depictions often found in movies and books.

> **WORDS IN CONTEXT**
>
> **fiefdom: an estate owned by a feudal lord that was farmed by peasants who, in exchange for their work, were provided protection and their own small plots of land for subsistence farming.**

During the ten-century medieval period, people engaged in age-old practices such as weaving cloth, growing and preparing food, brewing beer and wine, getting married, celebrating births, keeping clean, playing games, and other basic human activities. In addition, some of the great cathedrals of Europe were constructed during medieval times, including Notre Dame in Paris, built around 1160; Salisbury Cathedral, finished in England in 1258; and the Milan Cathedral, completed in 1386. These grand monuments to human creativity, which remain in use today, show that the medieval period was more than a time of plagues and warfare. It was also an incredibly rich epoch that laid the groundwork for modern society.

CHAPTER ONE

The Commoner's Table

During the fourteenth century the English author William Langland described food in the home of a peasant called Piers Plowman: "[Two] green cheeses, some curds and cream, an oat cake, and two loaves of bran and beans. He also has parsley, leeks and much cabbage, but no money with which to buy pullets [chickens], no eggs and no salt meat."[2]

The impoverished Piers was undoubtedly a serf, also called a commoner. Green cheese was not green in color but freshly made cheese that had not been properly aged. It seems Piers did not have expensive flour; he was forced to bake bread with bran, the hard outer layer of wheat or rye that is a by-product of milling. The loaf was extended with beans or lentils used as filler. Bean bread was usually fed to horses, but people would eat it when times were tough. With no chicken, eggs, or meat, Piers was among the poorest of peasants.

Serfs like Piers were at the bottom of a medieval economic structure called feudalism. The king owned all the land and sat at the top of the feudal system. He handed out land grants, called fiefs, to aristocrats. Known as lords, these aristocrats lived in large homes called manors. In return for the land grant, the lord was required to kneel before the king, swear his loyalty, and promise to provide military service. A serf was beholden to the lord and swore a similar oath to him. In return, the lord granted the serf the right to work a portion of his land grant.

The overwhelming majority of people during the medieval era were serfs who were bound to the land. The lord provided protection from sieges, invasions, roaming thieves, and other threats. In return, serfs turned over more than half of all their crops to the lord of the manor. Serfs were also required to do what the English called boon work; they had to work three days a week for their lord. In addition, most serfs were required to tithe, or contribute, one-tenth of their harvest to the church. The system was reinforced by a bailiff who worked for the lord and collected rents, managed the workload of the serfs, and even supervised their daily lives.

A Plowman's Life

Plowmen like Piers used heavy plows pulled by teams of oxen. The plows overturned the earth with curved blades called moldboards. In a text published around 1000 CE, a plowman describes his labors:

> O my lord, I work very hard: I go out at dawn, driving the cattle to the field, and I yoke them to the plow. Nor is the weather so bad in winter that I dare to stay at home, for fear of my lord: but when the oxen are yoked, and . . . attached to the plow, I must plow one whole field a day, or more. . . . I must fill the manger of the oxen with hay, and water them and carry out the dung. . . . [It] is a great labor for I am not free.[3]

Although oxen were cheaper to buy and feed, horses became more common around the tenth century and somewhat eased the burdens of the plowman. A new device, the horse collar, made working with horses easier. Imported from China, where it was invented, the padded collar fit around a horse's neck and enabled the animal to pull a plow or heavy cart faster than an ox.

Farm fields were narrow 1-acre (0.4 ha) strips of land separated by furrows, or trenches, which allowed rainwater to drain away from crops.

A team of oxen helps a farmer with the job of plowing while other workers sow seeds for the next season's crops. Those who worked the land had long days and little compensation for their efforts.

And plowmen worked close to home; their small, dark huts were surrounded by the land they worked. Fields were broken up by tiny villages where artisan and craft workers plied their trades.

When not plowing and harvesting, men dug ditches and wells, fixed fences, and maintained tools. Peasant women tended gardens, milked cows, preserved meat and fruit, churned butter, made cheese, slaughtered chickens and pigs, sheared sheep, and even brewed beer. Women were also responsible for child care and for weaving cloth and sewing clothes.

Hearth and Home

Most commoners lived in one-room homes constructed of wattle and daub, or mud plastered over a frame of sawed wood and heavy tree branches. Roofs were thatched, constructed from tightly bound straw or reeds.

A hole or vent in the roof allowed smoke to escape from brick- or stone-lined hearths. Most were simple cooking pits ringed with stones. Homes did not have chimneys until the 1500s, and peasant houses were dirty and smoky. Glass was an expensive luxury, so a home's few small windows were covered by shutters. Constant exposure to the smoky, smoldering hearth likely left most peasants hoarse and bleary eyed—especially in the colder months.

Nearly every peasant had an iron cauldron used to make most meals. The cauldron hung from a hook and chain attached to an overhead beam placed above the hearth. The chain allowed the cauldron to be raised or lowered so the cook could regulate the temperature.

Iron skillets were placed directly on hot coals. Earthenware pots were set to the side of the hearth, where they would not be exposed to high heat. Cheese and butter were kept in a cool corner in covered clay dishes. A mortar was kept for crushing spices, and ladles and spoons were used for stirring and serving. (Table forks were rarely used in Europe until the 1600s.)

WORDS IN CONTEXT

hearth: a brick- or stone-lined fireplace used for cooking and heating located at the center of a peasant's home.

Potage and Salt Meat

A typical peasant meal was a stew, called potage, cooked in the cauldron. Boiled meat was lifted in and out of the pot with an iron meat hook. Roasted meat was cooked on an iron spit over the fire. Small birds and game were wrapped in wet clay, buried in coals, and cooked slowly. In addition to roasting and stewing, meat might be pounded to a paste, mixed with other ingredients, and served as a kind of custard.

With no refrigeration, food preservation was an important part of the cooking process. Animals were not slaughtered until it was time to eat them. Any meat not immediately consumed was preserved by salting, smoking, or pickling.

Meat and fish were cut into thin strips, lightly salted, and air-dried to create a type of jerky. Butter and cheese, along with large pieces of beef, pork, and mutton, were layered in a small barrel that was packed with salt. Food preserved this way could last months or even years. Vegetables were pickled, meaning they were packed in a clay crock with saltwater called brine.

Herring, cod, and pork were the most popular meats for smoking. The flesh was cut into thin strips, lightly salted, and hung over a fire to dry slowly and absorb the smoke flavor.

Brewing Ale

Brewing a type of beer called ale was another common practice among the peasantry. Ale was most popular in northern Europe, which lacked grapes to make wine. Home brewing was a small-scale operation performed by women to provide for the needs of their families.

Ale was more important than water because most European rivers and lakes were polluted by human and animal waste; purified drinking water was unheard of. During the brewing process, water was boiled with wheat and barley malt, herbs, and flowers of the hop plant. Boiling killed harmful bacteria in the water, as did the alcohol produced during the fermentation process. Since tainted water regularly killed peasants, most men, women, and children drank ale like water throughout the day. (Children drank small beer, a drink made of ale mixed with water.)

Some enterprising women, referred to as alewives in England, brewed large batches of ale to sell to local villagers. These brewers were often more common than bakers. Records from the small English town of Halesowen in 1340 show five full-time bakers, all male, and twenty-five female brewers. In Exeter, Devonshire, it was recorded that almost 75 percent of all households brewed and sold ale. About 30 percent were considered commercial brewers because they brewed ten times or more during a year.

Medieval farmers had to make by hand the clothes, tools, and utensils they used on a daily basis. In 1912 British agricultural expert Lord Ernle (Rowland Prothero) described various tasks performed by commoners to make necessary items for their homes and farms:

> Women spun and wove wool into coarse cloth, and hemp or nettles into linen; men tanned their own leather. The rough tools required for cultivation of the soil, and the rude household utensils needed for the comforts of daily life, were made at home. In the long winter evenings, farmers [and] their sons . . . carved the wooden spoons, the plates, and the beechen bowls. They fitted and riveted the bottoms to the [cow] horn mugs, or closed, in coarse fashion, the leaks in the leather jugs. They [braided willows] and reeds into baskets for catching fish; they fixed handles to the scythes, rakes, and other tools . . . shaped the teeth for rakes and harrows from ash or willow, and hardened them in the fire; cut out the wooden shovels for casting the corn [grain] in the granary; fashioned ox-yokes and bows. . . . Meanwhile the women plaited straw or reeds for neck-collars, stitched and stuffed sheepskin bags for cart-saddles, peeled rushes for wicks and made candles.

Lord Ernle, *English Farming Past and Present*. London: Longmans, Green, 1936, p. 29.

Foods Eaten in Britain and France

The food eaten by peasants varied by region and depended on climate and soil conditions. On the cool, rainy British Isles, peasants planted cabbage, leeks, onions, and garlic in their home gardens. They also grew cash crops like hemp, used for rope and making paper, and flax, which was used to weave cloth. Chickens were kept in the yard while sheep, goats, and cows were held in community pastures and tended by village herdsmen. Women often journeyed together to local forests to forage for wild foods such as nuts, mushrooms, and berries. Domesticated pigs were allowed to roam woodlands, where they ate nuts and acorns.

Medieval peasants planted cabbage, onions, and other vegetables to provide food for their families. Many also kept chickens and other animals in their yard for eggs, milk, and meat.

France, with its warmer climate, provided peasants with a more diverse diet. An eighth-century manuscript called the *Capitulare de Villis* contains a long list of foods, herbs, and spices that King Charlemagne wished his subjects to cultivate. Sage, tarragon, parsley, caraway, and mustard were common herbs. Vegetables included cucumbers, pumpkins, lettuce, celery, beets, peas, carrots, cabbages, onions, and garlic. Kidney beans and chickpeas were popular legumes. Charlemagne also instructed commoners to grow fruits and nuts, including apples, pears, plums, peaches, almonds, figs, and cherries.

Rich, Abundant Spain

Diets were different in the warmer regions of southern Europe, where olives, wine grapes, and dates were important crops. Olives were introduced to Spain by the Greeks around the fourth century BCE. By the Middle Ages Spain's Andalusia region was one of the major producers of olive oil, and it remains so today.

In northern Europe olive oil was an expensive luxury. While aristocrats ate olive oil on bread, it was used as a sacrament in the Christian church. Olive oil was also used as medicine for more than fifty different conditions, including wounds, burns, infections, and problems with the teeth and gums.

Arabs from northern Africa and the Middle East brought rice and citrus fruits to Spain and southern Italy during the eighth century. The Arabs traced their roots to the Islamic cultural center of Baghdad. They were known for their refined poetry, music, clothing, perfumes, cosmetics, and food. An Arabic poet and musician named Abu l-Hasan Ziryāb was known to have introduced the Spanish to numerous dining customs that later spread throughout Europe. Ziryāb pioneered the use of glass goblets at the table and the concept of eating meals in courses, which progressed from soup to meat dishes and ended with sweets for dessert.

Around the twelfth century the *Baghdad Cookery Book* contained Middle Eastern recipes that influenced cooks across Europe. Recipes called for cutting beef or chicken into cubes and simmering the meat with fruits such as apricots, pears, and dates. This mixture was poured over chickpeas, rice, or lentils cooked with onions and garlic and seasoned with spices like cinnamon, ginger, cumin, and mint.

Recipes from the *Baghdad Cookery Book*, along with a wealth of food, made Spain a diner's paradise by the thirteenth century. According to King Alfonso X of Castile, "Spain is rich in honey, abundant with fruits, teeming with fish, well provided with milk . . . filled with deer and hunt, covered with cattle, merry with good wives, happy with an abundance of bread and sugar . . . and well stocked with oil and fragrant saffron."[4]

The Community Bread Oven

The abundance of bread was important to peasants, clergy, and nobles alike. Bread was the primary staple, and almost everyone depended upon it for survival. Then, as now, many types of bread were made and sold. Bread flour was milled from wheat, millet, spelt, rye, oats, barley, and rice. The flour was mixed with water or milk with perhaps some dried fruit, nuts, or beans added. Bread was served sliced, toasted, and with or without crust. It was added to stew and soup recipes as a thickener and used to sop up gravy.

Not all bread was seen as equal. Whereas wheat was considered the best grain, bread made with oats or millet was ranked as food for the poor, only to be eaten in years of famine. Rye bread was also viewed as food only for the poorest of country people. Barley was mostly used to brew beer. Barley bread was dark and coarse and used as a form of punishment. According to nineteenth-century French journalist Paul Lacroix, "Monks who had committed any serious offence against discipline were condemned to live on [barley bread] for a certain period."[5]

Although commoners grew grain, they could not easily process it into bread. Hard grains like wheat had to be crushed into flour at a mill. And ovens were not part of a commoner's kitchen. To bake bread, women visited communal ovens that were fired up with large stocks of firewood several days a week. The domed ovens were clay or brick, stood several feet high (1 m), and were more than 6 feet (2 m) in diameter.

Sometimes the community oven was a place of conflict. Thirteenth-century court records from England describe numerous cases in which bread was stolen and fights broke out. In one unnamed village, three

Because the average commoner's kitchen lacked an oven, peasant women usually used communal ovens for baking bread. Bread made from wheat was highly prized, while bread made from oats and rye was considered appropriate only for the poor.

housewives were baking when "a dispute arose between them about the loss of a loaf taken from the oven, and the old crones took to their fists and each other's hair and raised the hue; and their husbands hearing this ran up and made a great rout [disturbance]."[6]

Millers and Thieves

Because of its importance, bread was used as a means to tax the peasantry. Serfs had to pay the lord a fee to use the mill to grind their grain and another fee to use the communal oven. Lords maintained a monopoly on baking by prohibiting others from building bread ovens. They also passed laws against milling grain and baking bread at home.

The fees were only one of the problems medieval housewives had to endure. Millers who turned grain into flour were notoriously corrupt

"Calamity and Sorrow, Misery and Oppression"

Before Henry II became king of England in 1135, a power vacuum had allowed the nobles to seize power in some regions. The nobles initiated a tyrannical reign over serfs, whose misery was compounded by crop failures, disease, and starvation. The following eyewitness account by the archdeacon Henry Huntingdon describes the scene:

[Some] drew to the churches for protection, and constructing mean hovels in their precincts, passed their days in fear and trouble. Food being scarce, for there was a dreadful famine throughout England, some of the people disgustingly devoured the flesh of dogs and horses; others appeased their insatiable hunger with the garbage of uncooked herbs and roots; many, in all parts, sunk under the severity of the famine and died in heaps; others with their whole families went sorrowfully into voluntary banishment and disappeared. There were seen famous cities deserted and depopulated by the death of the inhabitants of every age and sex, and fields white for the harvest, for it was near the season of autumn, but none to gather it, all having been struck down by the famine. Thus the whole aspect of England presented a scene of calamity and sorrow, misery and oppression.

Quoted in Thomas Forester, *The Chronicle of Henry of Huntingdon*. London: Henry G. Bohn, 1854, p. 400.

and performed numerous tricks to cheat their customers. A housewife might bring a pound of grain to the miller and be provided with only half a pound of flour. Water was added for extra weight or poor-quality flour might be substituted for high-quality grain. Such practices even gave rise to a popular medieval riddle: "What is the boldest thing in the world? A miller's shirt, for it clasps a thief daily by the throat."[7]

The many milling and baking hardships faced by medieval women were described by eighteenth-century French social critic Edme Champion:

> What rendered these monopolies so odious was not so much the fixed tariff or the prohibition against crushing one's own grain with a hand-mill or between two stones, and baking this meal at home, as the compulsion to carry the [grain] for long distances, over abominable roads, and then waiting two or even three days at the door of the mill . . . or, again, accepting ill-ground meal . . . and enduring all sorts of tricks and fixations from the millers.[8]

Since the production of bread was so demanding, commoners often cooked a form of flat bread in the embers of their own hearths. Yeast, which makes flour rise into spongy bread loaves, was not widely used until the sixteenth century. This meant peasant bread resembled a tortilla, a thin layer of cooked flour. This was used as an edible plate, called a trencher, placed under other foods and eaten after it was soaked with sauces and gravy.

Hunger and Rats

While medieval life was difficult enough when food was abundant, serious famines occurred regularly. Countless people starved in France in 809 due to cold weather and poor harvests. The population of Spain was decimated by crop failures in 915 and 919. The eleventh century was marked by forty-eight famine years, and in the mid-1200s a combination of crop failures and massive rat infestations led to starvation and disease from Germany to Italy.

Even when times were good, people were constantly exposed to germs and disease. Thatched roofs kept out the rain, but the damp straw attracted insects, mice, and rats, which built their nests in the material. The dung produced by these creatures fell on beds, tables, and food, spreading sickness.

Despite such harsh conditions, serfs rarely left their remote villages. Local lords provided the only sustenance and protection available. Few medieval commoners considered leaving their familiar surroundings in search of better lives.

CHAPTER TWO

Castle Cuisine

Perhaps nothing conjures images of the medieval era more than the sight of a massive castle towering over a humble village. Castles were built on elevated sites and surrounded by moats and thick protective walls called baileys. The huge fortresses were occupied by aristocrats generally referred to as lords. According to Master Chiquart, chief cook to the Duke of Savoy in the fifteenth century, castle dwellers included "dukes, duchesses, counts, countesses, princes, princesses, marquis, marquises, barons, baronesses and lords of lower estate, and nobles also in great number."[9] The children and extended families of nobles also lived in castles, along with servants and armed defenders.

By the end of the twelfth century, Europe was bristling with castles—more than 675 in England alone and hundreds more in Poland, Germany, France, and Italy. Castles were built not only to hold off enemy invaders but also to allow nobles to keep an eye on the peasants who lived beyond the gates. Knights and soldiers kept watch night and day from the castle keep, the tall central tower that dominated skylines in most villages. This system gave lords of the castle unchallenged power over the masses.

Feeding an Army

Feeding the numerous people who lived and worked in the castle was little different than feeding an army; many castle inhabitants were men-at-arms, including knights, military engineers, horsemen, scouts, watchmen, and sheriffs.

The lady of the castle oversaw a sizable domestic staff made up of servants, lady's maids, nursery maids, laundresses, butlers, cooks, butchers, and bakers. Other castle staff might include accountants, messengers, musicians, teachers, priests, gamekeepers, blacksmiths, carpenters, barbers, and tailors.

Servants slept in castle attics and cellars and even on the floors of kitchens and stables. When day began they crawled from their hard beds and lit fires in the kitchen and the great hall, or dining room. Knights climbed up to the bailey to relieve the night watchmen. With the help of numerous attendants, the lord and lady dressed for the day in brightly colored tunics of blue, yellow, purple, green, and crimson. The clothes of the wealthy were embroidered, tasseled, feathered, and lined with fur of squirrel, lamb, rabbit, otter, beaver, fox, and sable.

Fond of the Chase

Castles were at the center of a regional agricultural system designed to supply the daily nutritional needs of nobles, staff, and servants. Food was grown by serfs on the land grants of lesser lords and funneled to the castle from across the realm. The agricultural system was overseen by a person called a steward, or seneschal. The steward supervised the lord's estate and fiefs, kept track of produce grown and livestock slaughtered, and ensured taxes and rents were paid. According to a thirteenth-century manual on estate management, the steward was required to make the rounds of a lord's lands once or twice a year "to see and inquire how they are tilled, and in what crops they are, and how the cart-horses and cattle, oxen, cows, sheep, and swine are kept and improved."[10]

Not all food at a castle was supplied by local farmers. Hunting was one of the prime forms of entertainment for European aristocrats. As chronicler Gerald of Wales noted in 1176, English king Henry II was obsessed with the sport:

> He was immoderately fond of the chase, and devoted himself to it with excessive ardor. At the first dawn of day he would mount

a fleet horse, and indefatigably [tirelessly] spend the day in the woods, penetrating the depths of the forests, and crossing the ridges of the hills. . . . Would to God he had been as zealous in his [religious] devotions as he was in his sports![11]

"Slay Him All Stark Dead"

Nobles loved hunting because it was similar to battle. Hunters blew on ivory hunting horns and wielded knives, clubs, lances, crossbows, short bows, and arrows. With hounds baying, they charged on their horses after wild boars, bears, wolves, and red deer stags called harts.

Hunting parties could be enormous, and many were organized like military expeditions. Henry II employed four well-paid huntsmen, four horn blowers, and twenty beaters who swatted the bushes with sticks to flush out game. The hunting party also fielded numerous dog handlers, archers, trained wolf hunters, huntsman assistants, and one man who was privileged to carry the king's personal bow and arrows.

Despite the size of the hunting party, the sport could be extremely dangerous. Hunters were slashed by razor-sharp boar tusks and bludgeoned by the huge antler racks on harts. As French count and hunting expert Gaston III wrote in 1379, "[The antlers of a stag are] fierce and perilous, for many times have men seen much harm that he [the hart] hath done. For some men have seen him slit a man from knee up to the breast and slay him all

WORDS IN CONTEXT

flush: in hunting, to drive animals out of hiding.

stark dead at one stroke so that he never spake thereafter."[12] Several important rulers were killed by stags, including Byzantine emperor Basil I (886) and English king Richard of Normandy (1070). Richard's brother King William II also was killed by a stray arrow while hunting.

Commoners were strictly forbidden from hunting. Poachers faced harsh punishments even if they were hunting to feed their starving families. Poaching penalties included castration, blinding, hanging, or being sewn in a deerskin and hunted down by vicious dogs.

With the help of their dogs, members of the nobility enjoy a day of hunting. Hunting offered a chance to hone one's skills with various weapons and at the same time experience the thrill of battle.

The Chief Cook

Harts, boars, ducks, geese, and other game provided a large share of the meat found on castle tables. And food was more than nourishment for the lords—it was also seen as a status symbol and demonstration of political might. The wealthy flaunted their fortune and good taste by serving foods many would consider strange in modern times. Aristocrats ate almost every type of roasted bird, from large herons, cranes, eagles, and swans to tiny larks and plovers.

Fish were kept alive in leather tanks in the kitchen. Fish dishes might include eels, minnows, salmon, pike, and a delight known as "jelly of slimy fish."[13] Boar heads were baked with the tusks intact, porpoises were served with peas, and swan neck pudding was considered a delicacy. Cheese, fruits, nuts, breads, and wine accompanied every meal.

With such an impressive array of animals to be cleaned, cooked, and served, the chief cook was one of the most important professionals working in a castle. The chief cook was in charge of the entire kitchen operation and also supervised several chefs who ranked below him. He oversaw the distribution of expensive spices such as saffron, ginger, nutmeg, cinnamon, cloves, mace, cumin, and pepper, which were kept in locked spice cupboards.

Nobles placed great trust in the chief cook. He was the first line of defense against poisoning, which was common among medieval aristocrats who continually struggled over politics, position, and power. Numerous kings, princes, dukes, and other nobles were poisoned, and sometimes the assassins were wives, sons, or other family members. Some nobles employed tasters who would sample dishes before they were served. But the wealthy also depended on their chief chefs to prevent food tampering by assassins.

Pantlers, Roasters, and Scullions

The chief cook supervised an extravagant number of kitchen specialists, more numerous than members of a hunting party. The pantler was the person in charge of serving bread and butter. Other staff worked as roasters, meat carvers, bakers, pastry chefs, confectioners, and fruiters. Kitchens were also filled with those who performed menial work such as drawing water and tending fires. Hauling firewood was a difficult job but totally necessary, as medieval food scholar Melitta Weiss Adamson explains: "[Any] cook, even the best one, would have failed miserably without an adequate supply of firewood to fuel the hearths and ensure that all the food was cooked to perfection. Ordered by the cartloads, dense dry wood was continuously hauled into the kitchen, either through the wide doors or perhaps even some big windows."[14]

The most numerous kitchen workers were called scullions. Their dirty jobs included cleaning fish and game, turning spits, scouring pots and pans, and hauling waste. Some scullions rose above their lowly stations to become cooks and master chefs. One of the most famous was the French chef Taillevent, who cooked for King Charles V in the 1300s. Taillevent is remembered for writing *Le Viandier*, the first-known cookbook.

A Decently Built Castle

During the second half of the twelfth century, English scholar Alexander Neckam wrote about his travels as he visited London and Paris and rode his horse through the countryside visiting peasant homes and nobles' castles. In the following passage, Neckam provides a general explanation of a castle:

> If a castle is to be decently built, it should be girded by a double moat. Nature must provide the proper site as the mote or mound should be set upon native rock. Where Nature fails, the benefit of skill must take over, and a heavy massive wall, made from stone and cement, has to grow or rise as an arduous task. . . . Small towers on this wall must flank the main keep [tallest tower], which is set on the high place in the very center of everything. On the wall let there not be lacking baskets containing huge boulders to be thrown down if the castle is strongly besieged. In order that the defenders may not be obliged to surrender, there should be supplies of spelt and wheat, and haunches and bacon, and other meat put in storage: sausages and entrails, meat puddings, pork, mutton, beef, lamb, and various vegetables. One needs a spring that flows continuously . . . and underground passages by which those bringing aid may move about without being seen.

Quoted in Urban Tigner Holmes Jr., *Daily Life in the Twelfth Century*. Madison: University of Wisconsin Press, 1952, pp. 183–84.

Food Sculpture and Painting

Like other head chefs, Taillevent was more than a cook and supervisor. He was also a skilled artist. During the medieval era the wealthy preferred their food to be served in a wide range of colors and unusual shapes. This required chefs to create culinary illusions by making sculptures from food.

Sculptures resembling green apples were made with pork meatballs that were battered, fried, and delicately coated with bright parsley leaves. Dried fruits, dates, figs, and almonds were strung together on thread and roasted so they resembled the entrails of the wild boar, a delicacy.

In a medieval kitchen, workers tend to meat roasting over a fire and other preparations for a manor house meal. Workers who cleaned fish and game, turned spits, and scoured pots sometimes rose to positions as cooks.

Ground meats, vegetables, and baked goods were formed into elaborate sculptures of castles, ships, and mythological scenes such as Saint George on a horse fighting a dragon.

Some of the most elaborate food sculptures made birds appear as if they were still alive. Roasted peacocks, which were tough and difficult to digest, were returned to their beautiful appearance as if alive. Peacocks were refeathered and served on a platter with their glistening green, blue, and brown tail feathers fully fanned out. Beaks and claws were sewn back in place. Similar techniques were used in a recipe Taillevent called "Swans Reclothed in Their Skin."[15]

While swans and peacocks were among the most extravagant dishes, chefs also focused on color. Food painting required the use of flowers, herbs, and spices to tint food blue, violet, red, green, yellow, and gold. Jellies and custards were commonly dyed red with beet juice, yellow with marigold flowers, or black with boiled blood. Pigs were painted gold with egg yolks mixed with ginger powder and saffron. One of Taillevent's recipes, a green eel soup, relied on crushed parsley and vegetable juice to provide vivid colors.

Color was also important in more common medieval dishes with names like white sauce, green sauce, and yellow potage. One meal served to aristocrats throughout Europe on a daily basis translates as "white dish," or *blanc mengier* in France, *bianco mangiare* in Italy, and *blanc-mange* in England. Whatever it was called, the dish was made with white foods such as rice, sugar, flour, goat or cow milk, and white chicken meat. The ingredients were blended and boiled down into a thick paste that was garnished with fried almonds and anise.

The Castle Kitchen

With the focus on feeding numerous people, castle kitchens were much more complicated than those in peasant homes. Kitchens were often free-standing buildings with thick stone walls and floors. They were separated from the living quarters to spare nobles the smells, noise, and sometimes dangerous fires that could spread to the living area. To prevent food from getting wet or cold, wood or stone passageways were built between the kitchen and the great hall where meals were served.

Since the wealthy often ate multicourse meals, large kitchens frequently featured several hearths; a noble's wealth could be judged by the number of stone-hooded fireplaces in the kitchen. Philip the Good, Duke of Burgundy, had six huge hearths in pairs lining three walls of the kitchen. Several hearths had built-in ovens for baking. The fourth kitchen wall featured a stone sink that drained into an outdoor cesspool. Kitchen waste was dumped into a chute that led to the castle moat and the water-filled trench was regularly cleaned by scullions.

Wine and Royal Estates

Castles often had several important rooms adjacent to the kitchen. The buttery was not where butter was kept but rather where ale was stored. Each castle household produced its own ale, hiring an alewife to brew with grain grown on the lord's estate. The finished ale was stored in "butts," or large wooden casks, in the buttery. The servant who presided over the buttery was called the butler, and his main job was dispensing ale during meals.

The bottlery was next to the buttery and was used to store bottles of wine. The bottler presided over the bottlery and served wine at dinner. This was an important job because aristocrats were particularly concerned with their personal wine supplies, often made from grapes grown on their estates. Charlemagne's bottlers worked closely with estate stewards, as the *Capitulare de Villis* makes clear: "Stewards shall take charge of our vineyards in their districts, and see that they are properly worked; and let them put the wine into good vessels, and take particular care that no loss is incurred in shipping it. They are to have purchased other, more special, wine to supply the royal estates."[16]

Good Wine and Bad

Henry II was also known for his fondness of wine, and he had unlimited access to some of the finest in the world after he married Eleanor of Aquitaine in 1154. Queen Eleanor was the wealthiest woman in Europe. She owned large areas of Bordeaux, considered the best wine district in France.

The "Great Goodness" of Hounds

Medieval aristocrats considered greyhounds, foxhounds, and bloodhounds as important to the hunt as horses. Dogs were used to flush, chase, attack, and take down game. Hounds were also beloved companions, as French count and hunting expert Gaston III wrote in 1379:

A hound is true to his lord and his master, and of good love and true. A hound is of great understanding and of great knowledge, a hound hath great strength and great goodness, a hound is a wise beast and a kind [one]. A hound has a great memory and great [sense], a hound has great diligence and great might, a hound is of great worthiness and of great subtlety, a hound is of great lightness and of great perseverance, a hound is of good obedience, for he will learn as a man all that a man will teach him. A hound is full of good sport; hounds are so good that there is scarcely a man that would not have of them, some for one craft, and some for another. Hounds are hardy, for a hound dare well keep his master's house, and his beasts, and also he will keep all his master's goods, and he would sooner die than anything be lost in his keeping.

Quoted in William A. Baillie-Grohman and Florence Baillie-Grohman, eds., *The Master of the Game*. London: Chatto & Windus, 1909, pp. 79–80.

Millions of gallons of French wine were sold in England every year. Henry II levied a 10 percent prise, or tax, on all wine that entered the country; he received one cask from every ten imported. This tax on wine became known as the butlerage because it was paid to the royal butler.

The best wine was kept for Henry's table, and the rest was distributed to his castles around the country. All members of the royal households were allocated 1 quart (0.94 L) of wine per day, slightly more than the amount in a modern wine bottle. However, wine did not ship well and often spoiled on its journey from France to England. When the French poet Peter de Blois visited Henry II's court, he was highly critical of the offerings: "The wine is turned sour or mouldy—thick, greasy, stale, flat and smacking of pitch. I have sometimes seen even great lords served with wine so muddy that a man must close his eyes and clench his teeth, [sour]-mouthed and shuddering, and filtering the stuff rather than drinking."[17]

The Evening Meal

While the wine might have been bad, Blois could not have complained about the service. A typical castle meal was executed with the precision

A lord and guests enjoy an elaborate banquet. Such meals were likely to include giant platters of sliced meats, soups and stews, and copious amounts of wine and ale as well as musicians and other forms of entertainment.

of a military drill. Before mealtimes, servants spread tables with damask linen cloths and set out steel knives and silver spoons. Highly polished dishes included silver cups and shallow silver-rimmed drinking vessels of German origin called mazers.

Meals were announced by musicians blowing on long trumpets up to 6 feet (2 m) in length. Diners proceeded to basins where they thoroughly washed their hands while servants stood by with pitchers for rinsing and towels for drying. Dining tables were assembled in great halls in a U shape with a platform, or high table, for the lord and his most important guests at the center. The floor was covered with rushes woven into mats that provided cushioning for guest's feet as well as absorbent and disposable carpeting to soak up dropped food and spilled beverages.

> WORDS IN CONTEXT
>
> **mazer: a shallow bowl used for drinking, carved from maple and decorated with ornamental metalwork.**

Once the guests were seated, a procession of servants began serving food with the pantler in the lead. He was followed by the butler and his assistants pouring wine and ale. Servants brought in soups and stews followed by giant platters of meat, sliced and skillfully arranged by carvers. The serving tables set around the perimeters of a great hall earned the name *groaning boards* because of their creaking and groaning under the weight of the food.

Between courses guests were entertained by minstrels playing music, actors narrating tales, and jesters telling jokes. After dinner, as cakes and pastries were served, knights and lords would take over the entertainment; refined gentlemen wrote poetry and songs and sang and played the guitar-like lute or harp.

As the evening wore on, nobles would relax in front of a fire while the servants cleaned the great hall and kitchen. Finally, a servant called a chamberlain helped the lord prepare for bed, brushing his hair, turning down the sheets, and stoking the fireplace in the bed chamber. The next day the lord might schedule a hunt or spend the day at business, handing out fiefs and honors. But as night fell, the lord of the castle could rest assured his army of servants had done their jobs while he had survived to rule another day.

CHAPTER THREE

Merchants, Mistresses, and Market Towns

For most people living during the early medieval era, life changed little from generation to generation. The daily lives of ninth-century serfs were little different than those in the eighth or seventh centuries. People were poor and isolated, and they did not own any possessions they could not make themselves.

Around the tenth century, agents of change arrived in the countryside in the form of traveling traders who wandered from village to village. Their horses and mules were weighed down with wares that appealed to peasants and lords alike. Merchants sold sewing needles, razors, soap, mirrors, incense, spices, dyes, leather, silks, gems, and furs. Many of these items were brought over land and sea from Turkey, Morocco, Egypt, Syria, Iraq, and China via newly established trade routes.

"Enterprise and Energy"

In the early days of trading, most villages were barely developed centers that housed religious officials or soldiers. However, by the eleventh century a commercial revolution was changing the face of Europe. As traders grew successful, they established weekly bazaars in thousands of villages. Some of these grew into what were called market towns.

Rural people flooded into market towns with dreams of cutting their ties to the land and getting rich in the process. By the twelfth century places like London, Paris, Florence, Venice, Hamburg, and Barcelona were growing at a rapid pace. Medieval historian Richard Barber explains why: "In the country it was almost impossible for a man to rise from being a serf . . . to a great estate. There, the order of life was fixed. But in the towns it was possible to make one's way in the world by enterprise and energy. If a serf ran away from his village and lived in a town for a year and a day as a citizen, he could become a free man."[18]

Social Centers

With the promise of freedom waiting in medieval city streets, market towns attracted a wide variety of merchants. Craftspeople visited on market days to sell handmade clothes, tools, pottery, and other goods created in their workshops. Local farmers, cooks, bakers, and brewers sold homemade food and drinks from carts. Others sold from canvas tents, temporary stalls, and even directly from the windows of their homes.

As a city grew, a market might spread over many streets, transforming into a central shopping district with permanent storefronts and restaurants. Specialty markets also thrived with large districts dedicated to a single product like meat, fish, cheese, or baked goods. Guillaume de Saint-Ton, the master butcher of Paris in 1370, had three large stalls in the city's meat market. According to journalist Paul Lacroix, the butcher was so wealthy that he lived like a noble with "four country-houses, well supplied with furniture and agricultural implements, drinking-cups, vases, cups of silver, and cups of onyx with silver feet. His wife had jewels, belts, purses, and trinkets . . . long and short gowns trimmed with fur; and three mantles of grey fur."[19]

Market streets acted as centers for social activity where visitors ate, drank, and watched sports such as horse races, ball games, and javelin-throwing contests. Markets were also cultural centers where poets and musicians, angling for a tip of a silver coin or a pint of beer, recited poems and sang songs. Puppet masters, portrait painters, and acrobats capitalized on the free flow of money and goods at the market.

A medieval market attracts eager sellers as well as buyers. On market days handmade clothes, tools, and other items could be found for sale alongside produce, homemade pies, and ale.

"Pungent Districts"

Medieval people considered market towns to be wondrous, and it was often stated that the streets of London and Paris were "paved with gold."[20] However, a modern visitor might be appalled at the smells and the filth. Medieval historians Frances and Joseph Gies describe the bustling French city of Troyes, where an international fair was held annually:

> The streets have been freshly cleaned for the fair, but the smells of the city are still present. Odors of animal dung and garbage mingle with pleasanter aromas from cookshops and houses. The most pungent districts are those of the fish merchants, the linen makers, the butchers, and worst of all the tanners [who cure, soak, and chemically treat cowhides to make leather].[21]

The Vienne River, which flows through Troyes, was used as a dump by merchants. They threw animal entrails, carcasses, and other garbage directly into the water.

Pollution problems were compounded by the medieval love of pork. In most medieval cities, nearly every household possessed two or three young pigs. These animals roamed freely in the streets, rooting through piles of food scraps, carcasses, and other refuse. Cities were also home to massive slaughterhouses where sheep, cows, and pigs were prepared for market. And contrary to the myth that city streets were paved with gold, the streets were strewn with human waste, cast out in buckets from front doors and windows. This flowed through open sewers, down streets, and into rivers.

In most cities, administrators passed laws forbidding butchers, shopkeepers, and householders from emptying their waste into the streets. These restrictions were largely ignored. As a result, typhus and cholera, spread by excrement in the drinking water, were major killers during the medieval era.

Swelling Cities

Although the death toll was high, urban populations grew at a rapid pace as people swarmed in from the countryside. At the beginning of the twelfth century, around ten thousand people lived in Paris. That population doubled in the early 1200s when King Philip Augustus built his palace there. The king also paved major roads and constructed the first covered markets on the right bank of the Seine River.

King Philip built new 7-foot (2.1 m) walls around Paris, topped with paved patrol roads and fortified with guard towers every 200 feet (61 m). Eleven gates were open during the day to allow the free movement of merchants and shoppers. The gates were closed at night to protect Parisians from marauding bandits and invading armies headed by local dukes and minor princes.

By the time of King Philip's death in 1223, the population of Paris had exploded to fifty thousand residents. The city was one of the largest and most important in Europe. By 1400 Paris had grown to include nearly two hundred thousand people.

Parisians consumed food produced far beyond the farms in the immediate area. The city relied on grain from the vast basin of the Seine valley, which stretched for more than 120 miles (193 km) northwest to the English Channel. In addition, Parisians consumed large quantities of other food, as Belgian scribe Guillebert de Mets wrote in the early 1400s: "They ate in Paris each week, taking one thing with another, four thousand sheep, two hundred and forty cattle, two hundred salted pigs, and four hundred unsalted. Similarly, there was sold each day seven hundred barrels of wine, for which the king received his quarter [25 percent tax], without counting the wine for the scholars."[22]

After recording the amount of food consumed, de Mets went on to note that Paris had more than four thousand wine taverns. However, historians believe de Mets was exaggerating, especially when he wrote that Paris was home to "more than eighty thousand beggars."[23] That number would account for more than a third of the city's residents.

> **WORDS IN CONTEXT**
>
> **typhus: a deadly bacteria-borne disease that killed thousands during the medieval era, with symptoms that include fever, red spots on the body, delirium, and gangrenous sores.**

Buying Groceries

Many Parisians were housewives who were responsible for shopping and cooking. Most set out first thing every morning to scour city markets for bargains. Purchases were made with silver coins called deniers. The average Parisian laborer earned about fifteen deniers a day, and much of this wage could be spent at a meat market. A fat capon (rooster) required six deniers, a smaller chicken cost four, and a large hare required twelve silver coins.

At other food shops, inexpensive commodities like salt and jars of vinegar could be purchased with a few deniers. Pepper was costly at four deniers an ounce, and sugar cost twice that much. Priced at eighteen deniers for a quart (0.9 L) jar, olive oil was among the most luxurious purchases.

A woman tends to her garden. Like people in the countryside, city dwellers grew their own herbs, berries, and fruits to supplement the food items found in shops.

Ingredients not purchased at the market came from backyard gardens that were common in medieval cities. Housewives cultivated herbs like basil, savory, marjoram, parsley, and fennel. They grew lilies, lavender, peonies, marigolds, violets, roses, and primroses and used flower petals as ingredients and garnishes. City gardeners also grew fruits and berries such as currants, raspberries, pears, apples, and grapes.

Schemers and Cheaters

Due to the importance of bread in the medieval diet, laws were passed to govern the price, weight, and quality of loaves. However, these measurements fluctuated from year to year depending on the size of the

A Merchant "Wont to Wander"

In 1112 a British merchant named Goderic had a spiritual encounter with Saint Cuthbert, who died during the seventh century. After the experience Goderic himself became a saint. The following story of Saint Goderic's early years as a traveling salesman was written in the late twelfth century by the Benedictine monk Reginald of Durham:

Aspiring to the merchant's trade, he began to follow the [peddler's] way of life, first learning how to gain in small bargains and things of insignificant price; and thence, while yet a youth, his mind advanced little by little to buy and sell and gain from things of greater expense. For, in his beginnings, he was wont to wander with small wares around the villages and farmsteads of his own neighborhood; but, in process of time, he gradually associated himself by compact with city merchants. Hence, within a brief space of time, the youth who had trudged for many weary hours from village to village, from farm to farm, did so profit by his increase of age and wisdom as to travel with associates of his own age through towns and boroughs, fortresses and cities, to fairs and to all the various booths of the market-place, in pursuit of his public chaffer [bargains]. . . . Hence he made great profit in all his bargains, and gathered much wealth in the sweat of his brow; for he sold dear in one place the wares which he had bought elsewhere at a small price.

Quoted in G.G. Coulton, *Medieval Panorama*. New York: Meridian, 1958, p. 318.

grain harvest. For example, in 1362 about 7 pounds (3 kg) of bread—or four loaves—could be purchased in Paris for fifteen deniers. A decade later, 1372 was a famine year when fifteen deniers would only buy two loaves.

Although officials determined the proper weight and price of bread, bakers schemed to cheat their customers. They did so by adding substances to bread flour that could be quite disgusting. Dishonest bakers added sand, dirt, cobwebs, and ashes to their loaves. Contaminated dough might also be baked into pies with various other repulsive ingredients. In one London case a baker was caught buying kitchen garbage from cooks and baking it into pies that he sold for good profit. When apprehended, the baker was subjected to the standard, if odd, medieval punishment. The cheating baker was seated in a sled and pulled by a horse through the city streets with a loaf of contaminated bread bound around his neck. Any peasant who saw this would avoid buying bread from the baker in the future. In addition to the loss of business—and the humiliation—the sled runners on the rough streets apparently provided a very uncomfortable ride.

Bakers were not the only sellers of tainted foods. The contents of milk, wine, oil, and ale were often cut with water. Cheese was soaked in broth to add weight. Stale fish was reddened with pig blood to make it appear fresher. Cuts of meat were inflated with air to make them look larger, and wet rags were stuffed into organ meats to add weight. In order to stop butchers from cheating their customers, laws were passed against selling meat by candlelight.

The Mistress of the House

Most city residents were poor. However, the expansion of markets and commerce created a new group of merchants who were neither rich nor poor but rather middle class. These were the first people in European history who lived very well by the standards of the day but were not as wealthy or powerful as aristocrats.

Many middle-class households employed servants, laborers, and other helpers. These workers were hired, supervised, and fired by the housewife, who was referred to as the head of the household or the mistress. Around 1393 an unnamed Parisian businessman, known as the "Householder of Paris," wrote a book of detailed domestic instructions for his fifteen-year-old bride. (Early marriage was a common occurrence

WORDS IN CONTEXT

mistress: during the medieval era, a form of address for a wife or "lady of the house."

in the medieval era.) The Householder referred to his wife as "dear sister" and outlined the duties of the mistress of the house:

> Know, dear sister, that . . . you must be mistress of the house— master overseer, ruler, and chief administrator—and it is up to you to keep maidservants subservient and obedient to you, and to teach, reprove [scold], and correct them. And so, prohibit them from lessening their worth by engaging in life's gluttony and excesses. Also, prevent them from quarreling with each other and with your neighbors. . . . Forbid them to lie, to play unlawful games, to swear foully, and to speak words that suggest villainy or that are lewd or coarse.[24]

As far as shopping chores were concerned, the Householder advised his wife to purchase the right kind of eel. This eel would have a small head, a large body, a white belly, and skin that was "fine, lustrous, wavy, and sparkling." The Householder noted that the best Paris goose sellers fattened their geese with whole-wheat grain and oats, not flour or bran. He advised that male hogs should be killed in November while female pigs should be butchered in December. In an aside on soup preparation, the Householder of Paris supplied some advice for keeping horses comfortable: "Note that flies will not seek out a horse that is smeared with butter or old salted grease."[25]

Working Women

"Dear sister" lived much better than any female serf. Most young women of the middle classes were fortunate enough to attend private schools where they learned reading, writing, math, and Latin. This allowed them to pursue their own careers or participate in the family business when needed. Women also took music lessons; refined ladies were expected to play the lute, harp, or other instrument. And according to thirteenth-century French poet Robert de Blois, women were encouraged to sing: "If you have a good voice, sing boldly. In the company of people who ask you, and by yourself for your own pleasure, sing."[26]

In addition to singing, middle-class women worked as teachers, weavers, lace makers, and even in trades more commonly associated with men, including carpentry, barbering, and saddle making. Married women often controlled the family's finances, paying bills and taxes, giving alms to the church, and hiring laborers. Some well-to-do women were philanthropists who donated money to build schools, convents, hospitals, and orphanages.

"Swilling, Gulling and Carousing"

Many city women supported themselves brewing and running public drinking houses. The first taverns in London opened during the twelfth century, and most of the proprietors were referred to in public records as brewsters, or female brewers.

Friends and neighbors gather in a Dutch tavern. Although many medieval taverns were less than inviting, they provided a central location for visiting with friends, sharing news, playing games, and conducting business.

By the 1300s London had countless businesses selling wine and beer. (Distilled alcoholic spirits such as brandy and whiskey were not common until the late 1400s.) Cities contained three types of medieval drinking houses. Inns were large establishments, often built inside houses formerly owned by aristocrats. These places catered to a wealthy clientele, offering wine, ale, food, and lodging.

At the other end of the spectrum, alehouses were small, informal places that sold ale brewed on-site. An alewife might operate an alehouse right inside her home or out in the yard, weather permitting. The third type of drinking house, the tavern, was not as large as an inn but offered beer, wine, food, and perhaps one or two rooms in the basement or at-tic for patrons unable to make their way home. What-ever the classification, all drinking houses were marked with posts called alestakes. These held up painted signs with business names like the Cardinal's Hat, the Sun, the Greyhound, and the Lion's Head.

WORDS IN CONTEXT

gulling: fooling or deceiving.

Medieval drinking establishments were often seedy, dirty, and cor-rupt. They were magnets for prostitutes, gamblers, criminals, and beer lovers called "malt-worms." The following description by moralist Philip Stubbs was written in 1583 during the Renaissance era, but it could just as well have described a bar in the medieval era:

> Every county, city, town, village, and other places hath abun-dance of alehouses, taverns, and inns, which are so fraught with malt-worms, night and day, that you would wonder to see them. You shall have them there sitting at the wine and good-ale all the day long, yea, all the night too, [perhaps] a whole week together, so long as any money is left; swilling, gulling and carousing from one to another, till never a one can speak a ready word.[27]

Escape from the Streets

Despite such descriptions, medieval taverns were among the only places outside of church where people could interact socially. Business was con-

The Great Northern Famine

As cities expanded during the fourteenth century, urban dwellers required more food than was grown in the immediate area. Residents in London relied on food sources from all of southern and eastern England. Much of the food trade in Italy was based on moving massive amounts of grain by boat from southern regions like Sicily, Greece, and North Africa to Florence, Venice, and Genoa.

During bad agricultural years the food system broke down, and people in cities starved. The great northern European famine began in 1316 when grain harvests from Poland to Ireland failed. This had a devastating effect on the burgeoning city of Ypres, Belgium, where workers produced fine wool clothing for aristocrats. About 10 percent of the thirty thousand residents of Ypres died of hunger during the first four months of 1317. The starvation would have been more widespread if not for the city's business owners. As chronicler Giovanni Villani wrote in 1317, "[The] cost of all foods became so high that everyone would have died of starvation, had not merchants, to their great profit, arranged for food to be transported by sea from Sicily."

Quoted in Michael Jones, ed., *The New Cambridge Medieval History,* vol. 6. Cambridge: Cambridge University Press, 2000, p. 158.

ducted in taverns, courtships were conducted, and marriages were arranged. People gathered at inns, taverns, and alehouses to share news, argue politics, and play darts, chess, and board games. In this way drinking houses acted as an escape from the muddy streets, smelly water, and other problems of medieval life in the city.

CHAPTER FOUR

Weddings and Marriage

In the late fourteenth century a merchant known as the Householder of Paris expressed his feelings on marriage to his new wife:

> I believe that when two good and honest people are married, all other affections, except their love for each other, are . . . forgotten. It seems to me that when [husband and wife] are together they look at each other more than they look at others, they come together and embrace each other, and they would rather talk with each other than with anyone else.[28]

The Householder of Paris's words remain relevant in the twenty-first century. But they were recorded at a time when many customs concerning love, weddings, and marriage were first being established. Some medieval practices have changed little; then as now people were married in churches, brides wore special wedding dresses, couples exchanged vows and rings, and celebrations were held after the ceremony.

Matters of Social Standing

Some aspects of medieval marriage were quite different than people are accustomed to today. Most medieval marriages were arranged by parents, oftentimes when their sons and daughters were as young as seven. And during an era when most people did not live past the age of forty, couples were married when they were very young. Brides could be married at age twelve, and grooms might be fourteen.

Like most other aspects of medieval life, a person's social standing determined his or her approach to marriage. Serfs living on a manor were considered legal property of the lord, who viewed his workers much as he did his horses and cattle. The lord might deny a man or woman the right to marry if he felt the bond would lessen his power over them. If a lord did grant permission for a marriage, he would demand a fine, called a merchet, to allow a couple to marry. The fine, sometimes paid by the girl's father, was justified because the bride would move in with her husband, thus depriving the lord of her labor.

For those in the middle and upper classes, marriages were arranged to improve the financial or political standing of the family. Girls were selected for the size of their dowry. This consisted of money, goods, and land that women were expected to bring to a marriage. As soon as a marriage ceremony was performed, the dowry became the property of the husband and, by extension, his family. On the male side, a groom might bring a family business or an aristocratic title to a marriage.

Because marriage was viewed as a business deal, detailed contracts were drawn up by notaries and lawyers. These writs specified the exact nature of the dowry and what type of property would be given to the groom. Fathers had to approve and sign the contracts; without a father's permission, a son could not marry and a daughter could not take control of her dowry. The legal forms, like the following from Newington, England, in 1289, demonstrated the nature of an arranged medieval marriage: "It is thus agreed between William de Toter of Warboruough on the one hand and James West on the other, to wit that said James will marry Alice daughter of said William, and said William will acquit said James . . . eleven marks and will give this James other chattels [holdings], as it is agreed between them."[29]

A lawyer and notaries prepare a wedding contract. Marriage in medieval times was considered a business arrangement and as such required all terms to be clearly laid out ahead of time.

A "Kiss and a Promise"

The majority of medieval people were poor. A bride's dowry might only consist of a few blankets or some pots and pans. Many couples simply got together on what was commonly called a "kiss and a promise."[30] This meant the couple lived as husband and wife while promising to marry in the future. This was likely due to the fact that a man might not wish to marry a woman until he was sure she could bear children. Heirs were viewed as economic necessities for peasant farmers who needed children to work the land. As English folklorist John Symonds Udal writes, "It has been the custom . . . from time immemorial that they never marry until the woman is pregnant. . . . When she becomes with child it is then considered a proper time to be married, which then almost invariably takes place."[31]

Rules for Weddings

The fact that weddings "almost invariably" took place troubled church leaders. Bearing children without marriage ran counter to religious teachings. This prompted Pope Innocent III to formalize rules for weddings in 1215. The pope convened the Fourth Lateran Council in Rome's Lateran Palace to make rules and restrictions, called canon law, relating to matrimony.

The Lateran council emphasized that both parties in marriage must consent to the union; one could not be forced into marriage. To prevent forced marriage, canon law required wedding ceremonies to take place in public with witnesses present. Clandestine marriages, or those conduced in secret, were prohibited.

If both parties willingly entered into the marriage, they were required to say "present vows." This was an exchange of promises "in the present" that included words similar to "I, Margot, take you, Hannes, to be my husband now and forever."[32] Couples were banned from making present vows in secret so they could simply engage in intimate relations.

Aristocrats encouraged public marriages for a different reason, according to history professor James A. Brundage: "The upper classes sought to make their marriages as public and as splendid as possible, not only as a matter of honor and social obligation, but also to assure that [dowries and] property transactions connected with the marriage would be honored."[33]

Blood Relations

In past centuries aristocrats often married family members, such as siblings and cousins, to retain wealth and power within their households. This his-

Clandestine Marriages

In 1215 the Fourth Lateran Council formalized canon law with regard to marriage. The following passage from the council deals with clandestine, or secret, marriages:

> [We] absolutely forbid clandestine marriages; and we forbid also that a priest presume to witness such. . . . [We] decree that when marriages are to be contracted they must be announced publicly in the churches by the priests during a suitable and fixed time, so that if legitimate impediments exist, they may be made known. Let the priests nevertheless investigate whether any impediments exist. But when there is ground for doubt concerning the contemplated union, let the marriage be expressly forbidden until it is evident from reliable sources what ought to be done in regard to it. . . . The parochial priest who deliberately neglects to forbid such unions, or any regular priest who presumes to witness them, let them be suspended from office for a period of three years and, if the nature of their offense demands it, let them be punished more severely.

Fordham University, "Medieval Sourcebook: Twelfth Ecumenical Council: Lateran IV 1215," March 1996. www.fordham.edu.

torically common type of aristocratic marriage was banned by the Fourth Lateran Council. Canon law stated a couple must not be related within four degrees; that meant if a bride and groom had a common great-great-grandparent, their marriage was prohibited. In canonical terms, the law was based on consanguinity, from the Latin for "blood relation." People could not marry if they were within four degrees of consanguinity.

If an engaged couple broke any canon laws, for any reason, their children would suffer. According to the words of the Fourth Lateran Council:

> If any persons presume to enter into clandestine marriages of this kind, or forbidden marriages within a prohibited degree [of consanguinity], even if done in ignorance, the offspring of the union shall be deemed illegitimate and shall have no help from their parents' ignorance, since the parents in contracting the marriage could be considered as not devoid of knowledge, or even as affecters of ignorance.[34]

European society regarded illegitimate children as outcasts and treated them cruelly. In addition, an illegitimate child could not bear his or her father's surname or inherit his property.

Making Promises

If a couple fulfilled the marriage requirements of canon law, they sought official permission to marry from a priest. The priest asked the groom, "Do you promise that you will take this woman to wife, if the Holy Church consents?"[35] After hearing the affirmative, the bride was asked to take a similar vow. The couple then exchanged rings.

During the next three Sundays, public proclamations, called banns of marriage, were posted in the church where the ceremony was to take place. Banns were also read from the pulpit each Sunday by the priest. These announcements informed the community that the couple was to be wed. The banns prevented unapproved matrimony; members of the clergy or the public could come forward and reveal that the couple was closely related, the marriage was forced, or one of the betrothed was underage. It might even come to light that the bride or groom was already married to someone else.

WORDS IN CONTEXT

consanguinity: Latin for "blood relation," the term relates to being from the same kinship as another person. In medieval times, people could not marry if they were within four degrees of consanguinity.

Banns of marriage were not abolished by the Catholic Church until 1983. As a result, for centuries priests began wedding ceremonies by stating, "If anyone can show just cause why this couple cannot lawfully be joined together in matrimony, let them speak now or forever hold their peace."[36] This line is rarely included in modern wedding ceremonies but it still comes up often in movies—for dramatic effect.

Dressing for the Big Day

The activities of the medieval bride and her female relatives and friends might be familiar to a modern bride. A week or so before the wedding, the bridesmaid took care of all the bride's needs, preparing outfits and making decorations for the reception. On the day of the wedding, the bridesmaid made a bouquet and helped the bride dress in a fine outfit.

A middle-class bride might wear a linen chemise, a silk tunic with a fur collar and cuffs, and a knee-length velvet outer garment called a surcoat, embroidered with gold thread. It is likely the bride's outfit was blue since that color represented purity in the medieval era. Around the twelfth century the custom of the bridal veil gained popularity. The tradition originated in the Middle East and was another symbol of purity. The veil was said to protect the bride from the evil eye—a wicked stare from a jealous rival that could cause injury, unhappiness, or misfortune.

Whatever her economic status, the medieval bride did her best to look like a well-made-up woman of the era. She likely plucked her eyebrows and the hair above her forehead to give herself a high hairline. The bride and others in the wedding party painted their faces stark white with wheat starch, ground lily root, or blaunchet, a cosmetic powder containing lead. The cheeks were painted rosy red with rouge made from beeswax and dried angelica leaves. Rouge was also used as lipstick and, for a final touch, the bride applied perfume made of flowers.

A medieval couple is joined in marriage. The color of the bride's dress, blue, signified purity. Bridal veils became popular around the twelfth century.

At the Church Door

After the bride was dressed, the formalities of the wedding took place. The bride and groom stood with the groomsmen, bridal party, and priest before the church doors. The backs of the betrothed were to the crowd of kinfolk assembled at the bottom of the church steps. The priest asked if anyone present objected to the marriage and read the list of items in the bride's dowry. The groom named his dower, a list of property that would pass to his wife in the event of his death. The groom then gave a gift to the bride that might include gold or silver coins or a ring presented on a shield.

Like a modern wedding, the priest asked the man if he would take the woman for his wife, and he answered "I do" or "I will." The woman was then asked for her consent. The bride's father or closest male relative gave the bride away to the groom, who took her right hand in his. Sometimes the bride and groom would make short speeches to avow their commitment to one another. The ring was blessed and placed on the bride's finger with the words common at weddings even today: "With this ring, I thee wed and with this gold I thee honor."[37] The priest then gave his blessing and the wedding party moved inside the church, where a nuptial mass was celebrated at the altar.

At the end of the mass the couple kneeled in prayer and a large cloth, or care-cloth, was placed over them. This was part of an ancient custom signifying that any children born to the couple before the marriage were thereby made legitimate. Finally, the groom was allowed to kiss the bride.

"An Uproarious Supper"

The wedding was followed by a reception much like those held today. Drink flowed freely, food was served, people danced and sang, and a cake was cut by the bride. In England a specially brewed drink called bride ale was sold to guests with the profits going to the bride. In addition to ale, the bride and groom drank spiced wine from a decorative chalice called the wedding cup.

Before the wedding the groom presented his bride with garters, bands of fabric that hold up stockings. This present was based on the traditional belief that the bride would be faithful to a lover who gave her garters. As the newlyweds were leaving the reception, guests would try to grab the bride's garters for good luck. In order to prevent the bride from being injured, she would throw her garter into the crowd. Sometimes excited wedding guests tried to grab pieces of the wedding dress as souvenirs. This led to drunken revelers ripping the bride's clothing to shreds. These

"Much Merry-Making"

Around 1170 the French court poet Chrétien de Troyes described the ceremony after the wedding of the royal knight Erec to the noblewoman Enide:

> In the great hall there was much merry-making, each one contributing what he could to the entertainment: one jumps, another tumbles, another does magic; there is story-telling, singing, whistling, playing from notes; they play on the harp, the rote, the fiddle, the violin, the flute, and pipe. The maidens sing and dance, and outdo each other in the merry-making. At the wedding that day everything was done which can give joy and incline man's heart to gladness. Drums are beaten, large and small, and there is playing of pipes, fifes, horns, trumpets, and bagpipes. What more shall I say? There was not a wicket or a gate kept closed; but the exits and entrances all stood ajar, so that no one, poor or rich, was turned away. King Arthur was not miserly, but gave orders to the bakers, the cooks, and the butlers that they should serve every one generously with bread, wine, and venison. No one asked anything whatever to be passed to him without getting all he desired.

Internet Sacred Text Archive, "Erec et Enide: Part I: Vv. 1–Vv. 22," November 1996. www .sacred-texts.com.

scenes might end in fights in which partygoers would bring out clubs, knives, and swords.

After the newlyweds left the reception, they would go to their bedchamber. But their short time together was interrupted at midnight, when guests arrived to drag the couple back to the party.

Not everyone approved of the drunken revelry at weddings. In the late 1400s the Dutch social critic Erasmus complained that many wedding ceremonies were "tumultuous feasts" where the bride and groom

> rise from the table to join in wanton dances until supper, where the tender girl cannot refuse any man, but the house is open to the whole city. Then the unhappy maiden is compelled to join hands with the drunken, the scabby, and sometimes with criminals who are more intent upon theft than upon dancing; in Britain she must even kiss with them. After an uproarious supper, dancing again, then fresh drinking; scarce can a wearied pair go to bed even after midnight.[38]

According to Erasmus, the party might continue for up to three days. As a result of this behavior, monks and other religious officials were forbidden from attending wedding receptions. In some places the ban extended to all pious persons.

"Separation from Bed and Board"

As far as the medieval church was concerned, marriage was forever; divorce did not exist. However, marriages could be declared invalid or null under certain conditions. The church called this situation "separation from bed and board,"[39] with *board* referring to food as in "room and board."

Several official reasons allowed separation from bed and board. In 726 Pope Gregory II declared that if a wife was terminally ill, the husband was free to marry another so long as he continued to support the first wife. Marriages could also be annulled if it was discovered that one of the spouses was already married to someone else.

Aristocrats often posed questions of consanguinity in order to leave a marriage. As the monk Peter Damian wrote in the eleventh century, when a rich man grows weary of his wife, he

> weaves a false line of consanguinity; he accumulates proofs to fabricate unheard names of ancestors, and appeals for evidence in sup-

port of this allegation to old folk whom he well knows to have long ended their life in this world. . . . Indeed, the laws are put up for sale, and money justifies the delinquents. Money sets the laws in motion, and the false interpreter bends its obscure sentences to his own meaning.[40]

A wedding feast provides an opportunity for family, friends, and neighbors to congratulate the newlyweds. Music, dancing, food, and drink make for a joyous occasion.

"Until Death Do Us Part"

While the wealthy used money and influence to invalidate marriages, the poor might simply separate voluntarily without the church's blessing. During the medieval era, however, the number of people leaving their marriages was low. Husbands and wives relied on one another for their very survival.

Marriages most commonly ended when one of the spouses died. Little wonder people celebrated weddings with joy and abandon. Life was exceedingly difficult and often short. When a couple reciting their marriage vows promised to stay together "until death do us part,"[41] this was not an abstract concept. Death cast a constant shadow on medieval life and could strike down the bride or groom at a moment's notice. As a wife from Bath, England, states in Geoffrey Chaucer's *The Canterbury Tales,* "Of husbands at the church door I've had five. . . . And all were worthy men in their degree."[42]

CHAPTER FIVE

Fasts, Feasts, and Celebrations

At the end of the medieval era, in February 1454, the Feast of the Pheasant was hosted by Philip the Good, Duke of Burgundy. Philip was widely known for his extravagant celebrations, but the Feast of the Pheasant was astounding even by his standards. Over the course of several days, hundreds of guests were said to have consumed 9,000 loaves of white bread, 4,800 gourmet breads, 32 barrels of wine, 800 chicken pies, 1,600 roast pigs, 1,600 pieces of roast veal, 1,600 legs of mutton, 600 partridges, 1,400 rabbits, 400 herons, 36 peacocks, and 6 horses. According to an eyewitness description of the Feast of the Pheasant by courtier Olivier de la Marche:

> The feast was a lavish affair: guests entering the hall had to pass a chained lion before taking their seats at tables decorated with . . . fountains, moving [theatrical scenes], and a pie crust containing twenty-eight musicians. During and after their meal, guests were entertained with similarly exotic scenes; a fire-breathing dragon flew over their heads, and a small boy mounted on a deer moved amongst them, singing a duet in which the deer took the melody line. Finally, the allegorical figure of [the Holy Church] entered, mounted on the back of an elephant.[43]

It can be assumed that the singing deer was actually a person wearing a costume and the fire-breathing dragon was a puppet made from cloth and other materials. And while it may seem strange to produce a pie crust that could hold several dozen musicians, giant pies were common at medieval feasts. Sometimes they contained live birds that flew out when the crust was cut. Other times oversized pie dishes held jugglers, jesters, and exotic animals.

Philip the Good's feast was a rally to organize a crusade to Constantinople, in present-day Turkey. The Muslim Turks had conquered the city in 1453 and had deposed the city's Christian rulers. Many of Philip's guests were nobles who belonged to a prestigious order called the Knights of the Golden Fleece. Before the feast began, the duke and the knights swore a solemn pledge on a live pheasant adorned with priceless royal jewels. The men would stop at nothing to recapture Constantinople for the Christian faith. Before the feast ended at four o'clock in the morning on the last day, dozens of dazzled and drunken aristocrats in attendance made extravagant commitments to personally fight the Turks or fund military expeditions to Constantinople. Within days, however, most recanted and the crusade never took place.

Eat, Drink, and Be Merry

The commoners who made up the bulk of European society could scarcely have imagined the extravagance of the Feast of the Pheasant. However, even the lowliest medieval serf enjoyed numerous feasts and festivals throughout the year, if on a much smaller scale. Most were based on the Christian religious calendar, which included many days of fasting followed by major feasts on holidays.

Medieval society and culture was guided by the Bible, which holds mixed messages about food and eating. On one side, the Bible is full of references to food. As Ecclesiastes 9:7 states, "Go, eat your bread with joy, and drink your wine with a merry heart." In the New Testament story of the miracle of the loaves and fishes, Jesus feeds five thousand people with five loaves of barley bread and two fish. Jesus also makes a promise to his followers in Luke 22:30: "Ye may eat and drink at my table in the kingdom."

Although eating, feasting, and drinking wine are sanctified by the Bible, it also stresses that the soul will be nourished if it is detached from the

Guests enjoy a lavish spread during a celebration of the Feast of the Pheasant. At the feast, which lasted several days, guests consumed thousands of loaves of bread, hundreds of chicken pies, and sixteen hundred roast pigs among other extravagantly prepared foods.

physical world. Such detachment often requires fasting; Jesus fasted for forty days while in the wilderness. And in Matthew 4:4, when asked to turn stones to bread, Jesus answers, "Man shall not live by bread alone." The Bible also repeatedly warns against gluttony, or eating too much.

Good for the Soul

The mixed messages of feasting and fasting played out in medieval society. The church required people to periodically abstain from food. This

Fasting and Fishes

During the medieval era people were expected to fast three days a week. This meant abstaining from eating meat and all animal products, including eggs, cheese, and milk. The reason for the ban on meat was biblical in nature and can be traced back to the story of Adam and Eve who lived in the Garden of Eden. God told Adam and Eve not to eat the forbidden fruit, the apple from the tree of the knowledge of good and evil. When Eve ate the apple and gave some to Adam, they were evicted from the Garden of Eden. This act symbolized the downfall of humanity. By extension, earth and earth's creatures, including all land animals, were flawed by the failure of Adam and Eve to refrain from eating the forbidden fruit. As a result, no animal born and bred on the land was to be eaten during fast days as a reminder of humanity's fall.

While some Christians thought bread and water were the only foods that should be eaten on fast days, more moderate views were prevalent. Religious scholars reasoned that fish were not of the land, so they had escaped God's curse on earth. By living in water, the sins of humanity were washed clean from fish. This widely accepted belief led to a booming fish industry in England and northern Europe, where salted, dried, and smoked herring was eaten by the majority of medieval people at least three days of every week.

was based on a commonly held Christian belief that divided the physical body, or "outer" person, from the soul, or "inner" person. When the outer person prayed and fasted, the inner person would receive spiritual revelation.

By around 1200 the church interpreted fasting to mean that everyone should abstain from eating meat and animal products on Wednesdays, Fridays, and Saturdays. The fast on Wednesday was meant to memorialize the day Judas accepted money to betray Jesus. The Saturday fast was devoted to Mary and the celebration of her virginity. Friday was the strictest fast day, in memory of the crucifixion of Jesus. Everyone was encouraged to observe these fast days except the sick, the very old, and the young. Medieval English scholar Bridget Ann Henisch explains why fasting was considered important by religious leaders:

> Officially, the Church took great pains to emphasize that fasting was merely a useful self-discipline. It was taught that everything in the world had been created by God, and every part of it was good. A fast was ordered not because food in itself was evil but because it was so necessary and so attractive to man that some form of abstention from it at certain times was considered to be very good for the soul.[44]

Ember Days

Some zealous believers only ate the bare minimum of food needed for survival. A fourteenth-century monk, Saint Bernardino of Siena, even tried to eat the sharp, prickly leaves of thistle plants on fast days. However, most who were denied animal protein on fast days ate fish, fruit, vegetables, legumes, nuts, and bread.

Many medieval cookbooks offered fast-day recipe alternatives to popular dishes. For example, *blancmange* was prepared with pike instead of chicken. Creative cooks working in aristocratic households would sculpt salmon to resemble pork chops and even fill egg shells with chopped white fish to mimic boiled eggs. In addition, wine and ale were not forbidden on fast days. Many people filled their bellies with beer when food could not be eaten.

Four times a year, on occasions called Ember Days, the weekly fast days were considered particularly solemn: just after Pentecost in early summer, around the Feast of the Cross in September, during Advent in December, and during the six weeks of Lent in late winter and early spring. The Lenten fasts were the most restrictive. Between Ash Wednesday and Easter, believers were limited to eating only one meal a day, at dusk. During the entire period, no meat of any type could be eaten, and the prohibition included butter, milk, cheese, and eggs.

With so many staples banned for so long, the church made an exception for fish. For most peasants this meant herring, which was found in great abundance in the North Atlantic Sea. The fish was easy to catch, salt, and smoke, and it remained cheap and plentiful throughout most of Europe. However, the wealthy were not restricted to eating dried herring for six weeks every year. Most aristocrats kept well-stocked ponds that provided fresh fish during the long season of Lent.

Stewing and Brewing

A frenzy of celebration occurred on Shrove Tuesday, the day before the start of Lent on Ash Wednesday. Every morsel of meat in a household needed to be eaten, along with eggs and other foods. As British writer John Taylor colorfully described it in the early 1600s:

> Always before Lent there comes a-waddling a fat, gross, bursting-gutted groom, called Shrove Tuesday. . . . He devours more flesh in fourteen hours, than this whole kingdom doth . . . in the six weeks after. Such boiling and broiling, such roasting and toasting, such stewing and brewing, such baking, frying, mincing, cutting, carving, devouring, and gorbellied gourmandizing [gluttony], that a man would think people did . . . ballast their bellies with meat for a voyage to Constantinople.[45]

This day of roasting, toasting, baking, and frying is now known as Mardi Gras, or Fat Tuesday. The holiday of drinking, gluttony, music, and parades is held in Netherlands, Italy, Brazil, and the United States, where the biggest Mardi Gras celebration is held in New Orleans. Throughout the world Mardi Gras is also known as Carnival, from the Latin phrase *carne vale,* meaning "good-bye to meat."

64

A customer checks the quality of salted fish before making a purchase. Fresh and salted fish could be eaten even during periods of fasting that were required by the church.

Easter Feasting

Lent ended at Easter, and the day was marked by feasting on foods previously forbidden. According to records kept by English bishop Richard Swinfield, during the Easter feast of 1289 a party of eighty people consumed 2 boars, 5 pigs, 4 calves, 22 kids (baby goats), 3 fat deer, 12 capons, 88 pigeons, 2 carcasses of salted beef, and an equal amount of fresh beef. This was washed down by unlimited beer and 66 gallons (250 L) of wine.

Having been denied eggs during Lent, the Swinfield party also consumed fourteen hundred hard-boiled eggs. It is likely most of Swinfield's guests were parishioners who brought the eggs to the party. They were following a medieval Easter tradition in which peasants presented their lords and local clergy with live chickens and boiled eggs as ceremonial gifts.

The modern tradition of the Easter egg hunt also dates back to the medieval era. Ancient records describe hiding hard-boiled eggs from children on the holiday. These were colored with vegetable dye, although the eggs of aristocrats might be ornamented with gold leaf.

Most people did not work during the week following Easter. But when labors resumed, the event was marked by a smaller celebration called Hocktide in England. This celebration of drinking, eating, and gaming marked the beginning of what medieval people considered summer, even though Easter most often falls in mid-April.

Summer Festivities

Summer was a time of unrelenting farmwork, but labor briefly stopped for the May Day holiday, held at the beginning of May. On May Day young people went out early in the morning and gathered blooming hawthorn flowers, which were used to adorn their homes. A maypole was set up in the village square and was decorated with garlands of flowers. Boys and girls danced around the pole and games were played. The day ended with the comeliest girl in the village being named the May queen and receiving a crown of flowers. May Day was traditionally a time of flirting and romance, and sometimes boys and girls would leave the village in the morning and not return until after dark.

Around June 23, a midsummer holiday called the Nativity of Saint John the Baptist, or Saint John's Day, marked another time of feasting and celebration. In the days leading to Saint John's Day, English farmers drove their sheep into ponds and streams to wash them before shearing their wool. Sheep shearing was followed by a feast described by sixteenth-century agricultural expert Thomas Tusser in a short poem:

Wife make us a dinner; spare flesh neither corn;
Make wafers and cakes, for our sheepe have been shorne.[46]

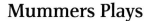

Mummers Plays

Mummers plays were performed by amateur actors on Christmas. The term *mummers* is derived from the word *mum*, which means "tight-lipped silence." The custom of mumming was not always perceived as a happy holiday tradition as medieval English scholar Bridget Ann Henisch explains:

> Mumming was a very old folk custom, its origins lost in the mists of time, in which a company of people, disguised by masks, animal headdresses, or simply blackened faces, made its way from house to house. Wherever the mummers entered they played a game of dice with their hosts, or offered presents, or performed a dance, all in complete silence except for some accompanying music. It was a custom associated with winter festivals and it must have been distinctly unnerving to hear the knock on the door and see a stream of grotesquely masked, totally unknown men pour in out of the wild darkness, over the threshold and into the hall.
>
> At some time in the later Middle Ages this folk custom was tamed, groomed, and transformed into an agreeable social amusement. Mumming by total strangers was frowned on, and many ordinances were passed against it because of the obvious danger that it could be used by the unscrupulous as a cover for robbery and violence. Mumming by known friends or respectable officials, however, was encouraged, and became a rather delightful way to make a call or pay a compliment.

Bridget Ann Henisch, *Fast and Feast*. University Park: Pennsylvania State University Press, 1976, pp. 222–23.

On Saint John's Eve, ancient traditions were carried out by revelers. Boys and young men were sent out to collect animal bones and other flammable rubbish. This was carried to hilltops and set on fire. The thick, acrid smoke was thought to drive away dragons, which were said to be afoot on Saint John's Eve poisoning springs and rivers. As the bonfires burned, wooden wheels were lit on fire and rolled down hillsides to chase off dragons.

After the fires burned down, the Saint John's holiday was celebrated with a roasted or broiled goose that might also be minced and baked into a pie. This was another holiday marked by excessive drinking, singing, and dancing. Wrestling matches and footraces were held, and villagers gambled their meager funds on the outcomes. A type of comical theater was performed where actors and audience members reenacted Bible stories with no efforts given to accuracy.

Saint John's Eve was held on the summer solstice, the longest day of the year. While most people in Britain, France, Croatia, Ireland, and elsewhere no longer believe in dragons, they continue to celebrate Saint John's Eve by lighting bonfires on hilltops on the summer solstice.

The Celebration of Wheat

Once Saint John's Day was over, the hot summer days ahead were given over to intense farmwork. Men, women, and children weeded fields, tended their vegetable gardens, and mowed, bundled, and stacked hay. There were few interruptions to the backbreaking labor until the August 1 harvest holiday called Lammas Day.

The church calendar calls Lammas Day the Feast of Saint Peter in Chains, but the festival was closely tied to harvesting the first wheat crop. On Lammas Day celebrants baked loaves from the new wheat and brought the bread to church, where it was blessed by the priest. This custom provided the name for the holiday: *Lammas* comes from the Old English word meaning "loaf-mass."

Like the dragon rituals of Saint John's Eve, the Lammas Day celebrations contained a touch of magical thinking. A farmer's blessed wheat loaves were broken into four pieces, and each quarter was placed in the corner of a barn. This was believed to somehow protect the grain that would be stored within the barn for the rest of the year.

In most years, grain stores ran low before Lammas Day, so when the first grain was cut it was greeted with great relief. In the days that followed the holiday, all of the workers in a village were called to harvest the lord's grain in an event called a bidreap. Although the work was difficult, there was a sense of celebration and hope that bread would be plentiful

Bonfires burn to mark the midsummer holiday known as Saint John's Day. The smoke from the fires was thought to drive away dragons who sought to poison springs and rivers.

in the months ahead. During the bidreap, lords customarily fed workers with meat, fish, bread, cheese, and ale. At some estates, a ceremonial harvest lord and harvest lady were selected to lead the cutting teams.

After the wheat was cut, the stalks were bound together in a sheaf and stacked in the field. On the last day of harvesting, teams raced against one another to see who would finish harvesting their section of the field first. The last patch of standing grain was cut with excitement. The harvesters threw their sickles at the plants, the curved blades cutting down the last of the wheat. The final sheaf was decorated with flowers and ribbons and was loaded on a cart. As it was hauled to the barn, musicians played, singers sang, and everyone celebrated with a final goose dinner.

"A Mess of Beef and of Bacon"

The harvest season lasted well into November for the medieval serf. The short, dreary days were marked by lesser celebrations, such as the Feast of Saint Michael on September 29 and Martinmas on November 11. However, nothing could match the excitement of Christmas, which lasted twelve days from December 25 until Epiphany on January 6. During this time the fields were wet and muddy or covered in snow. However, cattle, sheep, and pigs were freshly slaughtered, kept fresh by the cold weather. At this time of plenty, Christmas was celebrated by all, as Tusser wrote: "At Christmas we banket [banquet], the rich with the poor."[47]

Serfs prepared gifts for their lord, baking bread and brewing special ale sweetened with honey and spiced with cinnamon or other herbs. For his part, the lord provided a special Christmas dinner for his workers. One English account from 1314 states that a lord presented one of his serfs with "a mess of beef and of bacon with mustard, [a stew] of hen, and a cheese, fuel to cook the food . . . and two candles to burn out while they sit and drink one after the other if they will sit so long."[48]

After meals were eaten, Christmas stories were told and carols were sung by one and all. Carolers joined hands and formed a line or circle. Each person was expected to sing a solo verse. In some places festivities were punctuated by a procession of dancers holding torches and lighting up the night in a merry fashion. As medieval scholar Henisch notes, "Music and song, dancing and story, spectacle and surprise, these were magical ingredients that changed dinner into a feast, a simple meal into a special memory."[49]

Theatrical events called mummers plays combined all these magical elements. The Christmas folk plays were performed by actors and musicians called mummers and guisers (for the disguises they wore). Mummers plays originated during the medieval era in the British Isles. Mummers walked from house to house, and tavern to tavern, performing silent comic plays in which good characters fought against evil. Although no examples of medieval mummers plays exist, those performed during the eighteenth century would often pit Father Christmas against the devil or Saint George against Turkish knights.

Returning to Work

The twelve days of Christmas included New Year's Eve, but that holiday was not celebrated as it is today. The church preached that drinking and merrymaking on the last night of the year was a pagan practice, making it un-Christian. Most attended church on January 1, a religious holiday associated with the incarnation of Jesus.

Medieval people did hold small celebrations that marked the resumption of work after the January 6 holiday of Epiphany. This was known as Distaff Day in England. A distaff is a tool used to spin wool and was a symbol of women's work. On January 7, after the twelve days of Christmas, women gathered in the evenings to spin thread. Men called the return to work Plow Day and celebrated by decorating their plows with ribbons and playing pranks on one another.

While most work ceased on Christmas, when Distaff revelries were over, it was time to return to the hard labors of the land. With the church providing a progression of fasting and feasting days, the routines of life were carried out in orderly fashion for rich and poor alike.

SOURCE NOTES

Introduction: A Melding of Food and Cultures

1. Quoted in Melitta Weiss Adamson, *Food in Medieval Times*. Westport, CT: Greenwood, 2004, p. 98.

Chapter One: The Commoner's Table

2. Quoted in Adamson, *Food in Medieval Times,* p. 90.
3. Quoted in Fordham University, "Medieval Sourcebook: The Dialogue Between Master & Disciple: On Laborers, c. 1000," 1998. www.fordham.edu.
4. Quoted in Melitta Weiss Adamson, *Regional Cuisines of Medieval Europe: A Book of Essays.* New York: Routledge, 2002, p. 125.
5. Paul Lacroix, *Manners, Customs, and Dress During the Middle Ages and During the Renaissance Period.* London: Chapman & Hall, 1876, p. 110.
6. Quoted in H.S. Bennett, *Life on the English Manor: A Study of Peasant Conditions, 1150–1400.* London: Bentley House, 1956, p. 137.
7. Quoted in Bennett, *Life on the English Manor,* p. 135.
8. Quoted in Bennett, *Life on the English Manor,* p. 137.

Chapter Two: Castle Cuisine

9. Master Chiquart, "To Prepare a Most Honorable Feast," trans. Elizabeth of Dendermonde, Cariadoc's Miscellany, 1992. www.pbm.com/~lindahl/cariadoc/most_honorable_feast .hmtl.
10. Fordham University, "Medieval Sourcebook: Manorial Management & Organization, c. 1275," September 1998. www .fordham.edu.
11. Quoted in Thomas Forester, ed., *Giraldus Cambrensis: The Conquest of Ireland.* Cambridge, Ontario: Medieval Latin Series, 2001, p. 45.

12. Quoted in William A. Baillie-Grohman and Florence Baillie-Grohman, eds., *The Master of the Game*. London: Chatto & Windus, 1909, p. 47.

13. Quoted in James Prescott, trans., "La Viandier de Taillevent," 2005. www.telusplanet.net/public/prescotj.

14. Adamson, *Food in Medieval Times,* p. 60.

15. Quoted in Prescott, trans., "La Viandier de Taillevent."

16. University of Leicester, "Carolingian Polyptyques: The Capitulare de Villis," January 2008. www.le.ac.uk.

17. Quoted in Jay Williams, *Life in the Middle Ages*. New York: Random House, 1967, p. 2.

Chapter Three: Merchants, Mistresses, and Market Towns

18. Richard Barber, *A Strong Land & a Sturdy: England in the Middle Ages*. New York: Seabury, 1976, p. 41.

19. Lacroix, *Manners, Customs, and Dress During the Middle Ages,* p. 124.

20. Quoted in Barber, *A Strong Land & a Sturdy,* p. 40.

21. Frances Gies and Joseph Gies, *Daily Life in Medieval Times*. New York: Black Dog & Leventhal, 1990, p. 240.

22. Quoted in Jean Favier, *Gold & Spices*. New York: Holmes and Meier, 1998, p. 353.

23. Quoted in Favier, *Gold & Spice,* p. 352.

24. Quoted in Tania Bayard, ed., *A Medieval Home Companion*. New York: HarperCollins, 1991, p. 93.

25. Quoted in Bayard, *A Medieval Home Companion,* p. 114.

26. Quoted in Gies and Gies, *Daily Life in Medieval Times,* p. 255.

27. Quoted in Ian S. Hornsey, *A History of Beer and Brewing*. Cambridge: Royal Society of Chemists, 2003, p. 343.

Chapter Four: Weddings and Marriage

28. Quoted in Bayard, *A Medieval Home Companion,* p. 50.

29. Quoted in George Caspar Homans, *English Villagers of the Thirteenth Century*. New York: Russell & Russell, 1960, p. 161.

30. Quoted in Robert Dalling, *The Story of Us Humans from Atoms to Today's Civilization*. Bloomington, IN: iUniverse, 2006, p. 307.

31. John Symonds Udal, *The Dorsetshire Folklore*. Guernsey, UK: Toucan, 1970, p. 198.

32. Quoted in University of Oregon, "Late Medieval Canon Law on Marriage," 2014. http://pages.uoregon.edu.

33. James A. Brundage, *Law, Sex, and Christian Society in Medieval Europe*. Chicago: University of Chicago Press, 1987, p. 363.

34. Quoted in University of Oregon, "Late Medieval Canon Law on Marriage."

35. Quoted in Gies and Gies, *Daily Life in Medieval Times,* p. 265.

36. Quoted in Natalie Wolchover, "What if Someone Objects at Your Wedding?," LiveScience, August 8, 2012. www.livescience.com.

37. Quoted in Homans, *English Villagers of the Thirteenth Century,* p. 171.

38. Quoted in G.G. Coulton, *Medieval Panorama*. New York: Meridian, 1958, pp. 635–36.

39. Quoted in Homans, *English Villagers of the Thirteenth Century,* p. 173.

40. Quoted in Coulton, *Medieval Panorama,* p. 637.

41. Catholic Wedding Help, "Catholic Wedding Vows," 2008. http://catholicweddinghelp.com.

42. Geoffrey Chaucer, "The Wife of Bath's Tale," Florida State University, October 1994. http://english.fsu.edu.

Chapter Five: Fasts, Feasts, and Celebrations

43. Quoted in Adamson, *Food in Medieval Times,* p. 166.

44. Bridget Ann Henisch, *Fast and Feast*. University Park: Pennsylvania State University Press, 1976, p. 7.

45. Quoted in Henisch, *Fast and Feast,* p. 38.

46. Quoted in Homans, *English Villagers of the Thirteenth Century,* p. 369.

47. Quoted in Homans, *English Villagers of the Thirteenth Century,* p. 357.

48. Quoted in Homans, *English Villagers of the Thirteenth Century,* p. 359.

49. Henisch, *Fast and Feast,* p. 220.

FOR FURTHER RESEARCH

Books

Suzanne Art, *Early Times: The Story of the Middle Ages*. Yarmouth, ME: Wayside, 2014.

Frances Gies and Joseph Gies, *Daily Life in Medieval Times*. New York: Black Dog & Leventhal, 1999.

Samuel Harding, *The Story of England*. San Diego: Didactic, 2013.

Robyn Hardyman, *Horrible Jobs in Medieval Times*. New York: Gareth Stevens, 2014.

Gary Jeffrey, *Castles*. New York: Crabtree, 2014.

John Seven, *The Outlaw of Sherwood Forest*. North Mankato, MN: Capstone, 2014.

Websites

Crusades (www.history.com/topics/crusades). Hosted by the History Channel, this site features articles about the Crusades and videos with reenactments of dramatic events.

Food and Drink in Medieval England (www.historylearning site.co.uk/food_and_drink_in_medieval_engla.htm). A description of food and drink in the British Isles from breakfast to dinner to supper, with links to medieval topics such as the reign of King John, the Crusades, and the lifestyle of medieval peasants.

Gode Cookery (www.godecookery.com). One of the most complete sites on the Internet dedicated to medieval cooking. It offers recipe collections, a history of food and feasts, and pages dedicated to all the foods mentioned by Chaucer in *The Canterbury Tales*.

Internet Medieval Sourcebook (www.fordham.edu/Halsall/sbook.asp). This website provides a collection of documents written between the third and fifteenth centuries that describe numerous aspects of the medieval era, from peasant life to edicts issued by kings and clergy.

Medieval Life (www.medieval-life.net). Details of life during the Middle Ages, from England to Africa, are explored on this site with sections about food, famines, literature, history, health, and romance.

Medieval Life and Times (www.medieval-life-and-times.info/medieval -life). A comprehensive site with details about medieval art, castles, weapons, religion, history, food, music, the Crusades, and more. The section on medieval women describes the lives of everyday women along with queens such as Isabella of France.

INDEX

Note: Boldface page numbers indicate illustrations.

potage, 13, 14
    definition of, 14

Reginald of Durham, 40
Richard II (king of England), 7
Richard of Normandy (king of England), 24

Saint-Ton, Guillaume de, 35
Salisbury Cathedral (England), 9
scullions (kitchen workers), 26
serfs (commoners), 10–11
    definition of, 11
    diet of, 13–14
    nobles' tyranny over, 20
    poaching by, 24
sheaf, definition of, 68
Shrove Tuesday, 65
sickle, definition of, 70
social classes, 7, 10–11
Spain
    food in, 17–18
    foods eaten in, 17–18
sports, 35
Stubbs, Philip, 44
Swinfield, Richard, 65–66

Taillevent (French chef), 26, 27, 29
tanner, definition of, 37

taverns, **43**, 43–44
Taylor, John, 64
toolmaking, 15
trade, of foods, 45
trade routes, 7, 34
Troyes, Chrétien de, 55
Tusser, Thomas, 66, 70
typhus, 37
    definition of, 38

Udal, John Symonds, 49

Le Viandier (Taillevent), 26
Villani, Giovanni, 45

weddings, 53–54
    celebrations following, 54–56
    formalization of rules for,
        49–51
    See also marriage(s)
William II (king of England), 24
wine, 30–32
women
    careers of, 42–43
    as head of household, 41–42
    household duties of, 15

Ziryāb, Abu l-Hasan, 17

PICTURE CREDITS

Cover: British Library/Newscom

Maury Aaseng: 8

© Christie's Images/Corbis: 48

Thinkstock Images: 4, 5

Farmers plowing and sowing. Late 15th century. Italy./Photo © Tarker/The Bridgeman Art Library: 12

Peasant landscape (oil on canvas), Blanchard, Edouard-Theophile (1844–79)/Musee d'Art Thomas Henry, Cherbourg, France/Giraudon/The Bridgeman Art Library: 16

Fol.63v Baking Brown Bread, illustration from 'Tacuinum Sanitatis' (vellum), Italian School, (14th century)/Osterreichische Nationalbibliothek, Vienna, Austria/Alinari/The Bridgeman Art Library: 19

The Hunt in the Forest, c.1465–70 (oil on panel) (detail of 100861), Uccello, Paolo (1397–1475)/Ashmolean Museum, University of Oxford, UK/The Bridgeman Art Library: 25

The kitchen of olden days, English School, (20th century)/Private Collection/© Look and Learn/The Bridgeman Art Library: 28

Medieval banquet (gouache on paper), Jackson, Peter (1922–2003)/Private Collection/© Look and Learn/Peter Jackson Collection/The Bridgeman Art Library: 32

A Fair in Ghent in the Middle Ages (oil on canvas), Vigne, Felix de (1806–62)/Museum voor Schone Kunsten, Ghent, Belgium/© Lukas—Art in Flanders VZW/The Bridgeman Art Library: 36

Nova 2644 fol.49 r Picking Chickpeas, Tacuinum Sanitatis Codex Vindobonensis (vellum), Italian School, (14th century)/Osterreichische Nationalbibliothek, Vienna, Austria/Alinari/The Bridgeman Art Library: 39

Scene in a Dutch tavern, 14th Century (colour litho), Steelink, Willem II (1856–1928)/Private Collection/© Look and Learn/The Bridgeman Art Library: 43

Europe Middle Ages Costume, French School, (19th century)/Private Collection/© Look and Learn/The Bridgeman Art Library: 53

Wedding Feast in the Village (oil on canvas), Lancret, Nicolas (1690–1743)/Musee des Beaux-Arts, Angers, France/Giraudon/The Bridgeman Art Library: 57

The Feast of the Vow of the Pheasant (chromolitho), French School, (19th century)/Private Collection/© Look and Learn/The Bridgeman Art Library: 61

Fol.82v Salted Fish, illustration from 'Tacuinum Santiatis Codex Vindobonensis' (vellum), Italian School, (14th century)/Osterreichische Nationalbibliothek, Vienna, Austria/Alinari/The Bridgeman Art Library: 65

Midsummer Fire (oil on canvas), Astrup, Nikolai (1880–1928)/Private Collection/Photo © O. Vaering/The Bridgeman Art Library: 69